Who's Been Sleeping in My Bed(room)?

Researching a St. Louis County, Missouri Home

Kim Wolterman

To Sandy,
Autta friend and awesome cookie mamma!
Kim Wolterman

Provenance
Publishing LLC

provenancepublishing.net

Who's Been Sleeping in My Bed(room)?
Researching a St. Louis County, Missouri Home

Published by

213 S. Maple Ave.
St. Louis, MO 63119
314-283-4605
info@provenancepublishing.net
www.provenancepublishing.net

Library of Congress Control Number: 2009908373

10 digit ISBN 0-9824640-0-2
13 digit ISBN 978-0-9824640-0-7

Cover and interior design by Nehmen-Kodner
Copy editing by Christine Frank & Associates

Dedication

This book is dedicated in loving memory of my parents,
Roy and Catherine Kubler, who instilled in me
a lifelong love of books and learning.

Acknowledgments

This book has been many years in the making, and would not have been possible without the help and guidance I got along the way. First and foremost, I am grateful to Holly Ann Burt for sharing the Morton family history and memorabilia with me. Her past is my present.

I would also like to thank Bobbi Linkemer, who believed in my book from the first time she asked the question, "What's your book about?" Teacher and book coach extraordinaire, her prompting and prodding kept me on track with the book. My sincere appreciation goes out to my fellow writing Pashminas for their faith that I could and should write this book. A special thanks to Sandy Shaw for her Colossal Cookies, designed to inspire even the most reluctant of the writing muses.

Several people provided insight into the many resources available to house researchers in St. Louis County. Thanks to Ann Carter Fleming, CG, CGL and Ruth Ann Hager, CGRS, CGL for their genealogical perspective on the research; and Dennis Northcott of the Missouri History Museum Library and Research Center and Joyce Loving of the St. Louis County Library for review of the materials available at their facilities. I am also grateful to Edna Gravenhorst, St. Louis City researcher and author, for her input and support.

Thanks to Christine Frank for her editing services, and Carol and David Nicklaus for their additional review of the final draft of the book. And for her creativity and flair, I particularly want to acknowledge Peggy Nehmen for coming up with a wonderful cover and layout design for the book.

Finally, much gratitude to my husband Jim… just because.

Table of Contents

Preface

Obtaining a century home plaque for my house. It seemed a simple enough goal. All I needed were two pieces of documentation to prove the house was built in 1902. Surely a quick trip to my local historical society office would provide the necessary information. Right? Not exactly. It took three years and countless trips to multiple libraries, historical societies, the county government center and, ultimately, a trip to Chicago, before I was finally able to apply for my plaque.

Who's Been Sleeping in My Bed(room)? is designed to give the reader what I didn't have – a systematic plan to follow in researching a property in St. Louis County, Missouri. The intent is to remove the frustration and put the fun into the endeavor. When the reader runs into brick walls (sometimes, literally!), the book will provide other avenues to explore.

There is a huge interest in the documentation and preservation of historic structures in the United States. Some of this interest comes from owners who are applying for historical building status. Others are seeking to understand the previous owners and why certain modifications were made to their homes. Additionally, there is a growing desire on the part of many genealogists to find out where their ancestors lived and what their neighborhoods were like at the time they lived there.

There are a number of books available on researching house history. Most are not very current, and none of them is specific to St. Louis County. While some of the research areas covered in this book are the same as in existing books, *Who's Been Sleeping in My Bed(room)?* provides researchers with a step-by-step guide on where to find local resources. Further, the book contains valuable worksheets and reference guides to aid in logging information and keeping track of areas already researched, as well as a glossary to help define the sometimes unfamiliar terminology used in the legal document part of the research.

Introduction

I f you are reading this book, you probably own an historic home. But someone owned it before you. You may be interested in researching the history of your house for many reasons. It may be that you are restoring or rehabilitating an old house. Maybe you are seeking historic designation for the property. Perhaps you want to obtain a century home plaque from your local historical society. Or you might be among the growing number of genealogists who want to find out about an ancestor's home.

Whatever your motivation, learning about an old house and its history can be interesting and rewarding. It can also be frustrating. Often people do not know where to go to obtain information helpful to their research. Typically there is no one location that contains all the records necessary to complete your search. This book will provide you with a systematic approach to your research, offering information and tools that you can use to learn more about the house you are investigating. Its purpose is to guide you through the sometimes baffling maze of county, municipal and other records to those that are the most likely to contain pertinent information for compiling a house history. It will also direct you to those libraries and archives in St. Louis County that hold significant collections of books, newspapers, or manuscripts from which more information might be obtained.

You may exhaust all the possible avenues and still not find answers to your questions. But no matter what the end result, you will still uncover some interesting information about your house and the community it was built in.

Documenting house history is more than just writing down names and dates. Your completed research will paint a picture of life in the past in your home and neighborhood. Not only will this be of interest to you, but future home-owners and genealogists will treasure your findings and be able to add to them as well.

So, have fun and good luck!

213 S. Maple Avenue, Circa 1902.

Section One:
Let's Start at the Very Beginning

Organizing Your Research

The first step is to decide how you will organize the information you obtain. There is nothing more frustrating than trying to find a scrap of paper that you know you took notes on – unless it is going over ground you have already covered because you can't remember which sources you have looked at in the past. Because most people will do the research over a period of months, or even years, it is impossible to remember what has been done without an organized file.

• *Filing Your Information*

During my research, I found it helpful to use a three ring binder with dividers separating the various sources of research such as directories, title searches, and correspondence. If all notes are made on 8½" x 11" sheets of paper they can then be easily inserted into the proper section of the binder. Writings on small scraps of paper tend to get lost. If you do make a note on a smaller piece of paper, copy it onto an 8½" x 11" sheet of paper later. Most photocopies made during the search process will be this size, making everything consistent and easy to file.

A binder with dividers will keep all of your notes organized.

• *Recording Information*

Record information as soon as you find it and write down, in detail, where and when a search was made. Keep track of everything you look at, even those items that contain no useful information. Write down the source by author and title, or the file number if that is how the institution listed it. Also note any contacts you make, whether by letter, phone, email or in person. The Research Log located in Appendix II on pages 46-47 and Correspondence Log located in Appendix II on pages 48-49 will aid you in your documentation efforts. You will be able to see at a glance which resources you have already re-viewed. The Research Log can also help you plan future trips as well. You can list the sources you wish to review when you go to the library, courthouse, etc. and note the call or microfilm numbers so you save time once you are at the repository.

Keep a Research Log for all of your online research as well. Again, you don't want to keep revisiting web sites you have already checked in the past.

- ### *Start a Research To-Do List*

Organize your research tasks in an efficient and logical fash-
ion. Decide what you need to know and where you can find it.
Using the Research To-Do List in Appendix II on pages 50-51,
make a list of specific tasks, noting where you need to go, to
whom you need to speak, what you expect to find, and the
order in which you intend to proceed. You can modify this list
as you proceed with your research.

- ### *Use Archival Safe Materials*

As you begin to accumulate photos, documents and newspaper
clippings, make certain that all of your copies are made on
archival-quality paper. All storage boxes and binder sleeves
should be archival safe as well. Before storing photos, label
each one with a photo-safe marking pencil, noting the date,
location and any subjects in the photo.

Key

*A quick Internet search for archival safe materials will yield
dozens of sources for paper, pens, boxes, etc.*

How Old *Is* This Old House?

If you are the owner of the house, you may have received an
informational sheet from the realtor when you first looked at
your house. Almost always these sheets contain a date indicat-
ing when the house was built. While it is definitely useful in
narrowing down a construction date, don't assume the date is
accurate. The same is true with the date St. Louis County has
on record as being the age of your house. Use this date as a
starting point, but search for documents to prove its legitimacy.

- **_Walk the Property_**

Before heading off to look through records, start with what is
right in front of you. The property itself is a primary source of
information. With a notebook and pen in hand, walk the entire
property. Take a close look at all buildings and structures,
inside as well as out, noting distinctive features and obvious
alterations and changes. Look for evidence of previous buildings, roadways, paths, fences, and other features. The style of
a building is a clue to its age, as are the materials used in
construction. Some homeowners have found newspapers
that were used as insulation, helping to date the structure. The
foundation material, types of nails used, and even the style of
home can help to establish a construction date. Several
good books on architectural clues and styles are listed in the
bibliography.

- **_Interview Prior Homeowners/Neighbors_**

A second source of information, useful for both the genealogist
and the homeowner, is current neighbors. They may be able to
provide additional historical information about the house. Look
for the long-term residents, and ask about renovations they
observed and about other owners of the property. If you are
able to locate previous owners, try to interview them about
what they know of the house history, what it was like to live
in the house, or any fond memories they have. They may even
share some photographs or old architectural plans with you.
If you can talk to them at the house, you may find that being
in their old home elicits some additional memories. A tape
recorder can help ensure that you don't miss anything, but get
the permission of the person being interviewed first. Have your

questions prepared before the interview, and use open-ended questions to get the conversation flowing. Try to avoid those that will result in simple "yes" or "no" answers.

Gathering as much information as you can from the home itself, as well as from neighbors and previous owners, can help guide you to the next logical step in your research. It may also provide you with some great background material that can't be found in books or records.

Brief History of St. Louis County

Even though the home you are researching is located in St. Louis County, it is important to understand a little bit of the history of the county in order to ascertain where the records you need will be located. While the City of St. Louis was founded in 1764, St. Louis County did not come into existence until 1812. At this point St. Louis County included the City of St. Louis. The county seat was the City of St. Louis, so all records for both the county and the city were housed here. In 1876 the citizens of St. Louis County, which included residents of both the city and the county, voted that the City of St. Louis should separate from the county and become independent. In 1877, St. Louis County began its own government and to maintain its own records.

Key

During the transition years of 1877 and 1878, look for records in both the city and the county as the newly built St. Louis County Courthouse was not occupied until the end of 1878.

1878 Map.

Section Two: Searching the Records

Things to Know Before You Go to a Research Center

• *Obtain the Property's Legal Description*

The very first thing that you need to have is a legal description
of the property. If you are the homeowner, this can be obtained
by looking at the deed you received when you purchased the
property. If you can't locate the deed, look on the assessment
notice you receive from St. Louis County. If you are not the
homeowner, the St. Louis County Department of Revenue's
website at **http://revenue.stlouisco.com/ias/** contains real
estate information. Enter the address you are researching
in the lower left corner and click "Find". The Locator ID will
appear on the lower center section of the screen. Click on the
Locator ID, and the Ownership/Legal Information will be
displayed, including the legal description. This legal description will identify the property you are researching so that
when you are looking through records you can make certain
you are dealing with the correct property. One of my property
owners, for example, owned multiple pieces of land in Webster
Groves. Without the legal description I might have spent time
researching the wrong piece of property.

1998081201042

DANIEL T. O'LEARY
RECORDER OF DEEDS
ST. LOUIS COUNTY MISSOURI
41 SOUTH CENTRAL
CLAYTON, MO 63105

RECORDER OF DEEDS DOCUMENT IDENTIFICATION & CERTIFICATION SHEET

TYPE OF INSTRUMENT	GRANTOR	TO	GRANTEE
WD	G STAFFORD CO	W L S 7722 L L C	

PROPERTY DESCRIPTION: SHREWSBURY PARK 1 LOT 12 BLK 3 PB 3 PG 7

Lien Number	Notation	Document Number	Locator
		1,042	22J131772

STATE OF MISSOURI)
) SS.
COUNTY OF ST. LOUIS)

I, the undersigned Recorder of Deeds for said County and State, do hereby certify that the following and annexed instrument of writing, which consists of ___3___ pages, (this page inclusive), was filed for record in my office on the ___12___ day of ___August___ ___1998___ at ___02:24 PM___ and is truly recorded in the book and at the page shown at the top and/or bottom of this page.

In witness whereof I have hereunto set my hand and official seal the day, month and year aforesaid.

Recorder of Deeds
St. Louis County, Missouri

Deputy Recorder

RECORDING FEE ___$21.00___

(Paid at the time of Recording)

This document provides a legal description of the property.

• *Contact Research Facilities Prior to Visit*

Contact all organizations and institutions you intend to visit ahead of time. Write down the questions you want to ask before you make your initial contact, utilizing the Research To-Do List in Appendix II on pages 50-51. When you call, explain exactly what you are hoping to accomplish. Inquire about the hours and procedures for using special collections, archives, and other records. Be sure to ask about parking availability and cost, as well as photocopy fees.

• *Talk to the Staff*

When you arrive at the research center, talk to the staff, especially reference people, archivists, and librarians. Let them know what you are working on. They may have additional suggestions for you in terms of resources at their facility or other facilities in the area. It will be helpful to bring your notebook, pencils (some libraries may not allow you to bring in pens), magnifying glass, small stapler, coins for photocopies, and tracing paper in case you come across a map that cannot be photocopied. Many facilities will allow you to take digital photographs, so a camera may come in handy. Lastly, bring photos of your house. You may be lucky enough to come across someone with enough historical construction background to give you an estimate on the construction date.

Abstract of Title

If you are an extremely lucky homeowner, you received an abstract of title for the property when you bought your house. Also referred to as a chain of title, an abstract contains a legal description of the property, as well as all transactions on the property back to the patentee – the original purchaser of the

Chain of Title for 213 S. Maple Avenue.

Chain of Title Example

St. Louis Co. Deed Book	Page	Date	Description
231 *	347	1867	Joseph Ridgway sold to John R. Shepley - 20 acres
032	65	05/26/1886	Mary A. Shepley (of St. Louis City) sold to Alexander Russell (of Webster Groves) - 20 acres *Deed* Price: $9,200.00
056	253	11/01/1890	Alexander Russell (of St. Louis County) sold to David H. Hays (of St. Louis County) - Lot 16 *Deed* Price: $1,200.00
056	254	11/01/1890	David & Clifton B. Hays (of St. Louis County) sold to John B. Pratt (of St. Louis City) - Lot 16 *General Warranty Deed/Indenture* Price: $1,200.00
120	140	07/26/1900	John B. Pratt (a single man of St. Louis Co.) sold to David W. Graham (of St. Louis Co.) - Lot 16 *Indenture* Price: $2,000.00
120	141	07/26/1900	David W. and Mary McD Graham (parties of the 1st part, John Gibson (party of the 2nd part) and John B. Pratt (party of the 3rd part) *Deed of Trust* - due in 3 years
123	312	08/04/1900	Berry Horn Coal Company *Quit Claim* to the Grahams. Payment: $15.00, Release from judgment (Book 4, Page 58) dated 10/22/1898 for $55.59 interest and costs.
122	441	02/07/1901	David W. & Mary McD. Graham (of St. Louis Co.) sold to Charles A. & Julia A. Stelle, (of Greene Co., IL.) *General Warranty Deed* Price: $1.00 and other consideration
124	504	04/22/1901	Charles A. & Julia A. Stelle (of Greene Co., IL) sold to George D. Barnett (of St. Louis City) *Indenture* Price: $2,200.00, plus Pratt loan
133	017	04/01/1902	George D. & Nellie R. Barnett (of St. Louis City) sold to Claude A. & Jessie G. Morton (of St. Louis City) *Warranty Deed* Price: $1,650.00, plus Pratt loan
1506	495	08/06/1938	Claude A. & Jessie G. Morton (of St. Louis Co.) sold to Arthur W. & Hazel A. Lindholm (of St. Louis Co.) *General Warranty Deed* Price: $100.00 and other consideration
1748	034	07/25/1940	Arthur W. & Hazel A. Lindholm sold south half of Lot 16 to Beata & Agnes Lindholm *General Warranty Deed* Price: $10.00 and other consideration
8168	1070	07/17/1987	Hazel A. Lindholm sold to James J. & Kimberly A. Wolterman *Warranty Deed* Price: $1.00 and other consideration

* City of St. Louis Deed Book

property from the federal government. References to deeds, mortgages, wills, probate records, divorces, and lawsuits may be included in the abstract. In the past, abstracts were routinely prepared and updated by the owner's mortgage company each time a home changed hands. This practice went by the wayside when title insurance began to replace abstracts in the 1970s. If there is no abstract, you will need to form a chain of title through other records.

Most chain of title searches will begin at the St. Louis County Recorder of Deeds Division, which is located on the fourth floor of the Lawrence K. Roos County Government Building, 41 S. Central Avenue, Clayton, Missouri. This office has records and files instruments of writing affecting real property or personal property. It is here that you will find the deeds for all property in St. Louis County from the present back to 1877. Remember that all records prior to 1877 are housed in the Recorder of Deeds office, St. Louis City Hall, 1200 Market Street in room 126. Deeds from 1764 forward are located in City Hall. Prior to 1804, there were French and Spanish Land Grants, which have been filmed and are available at the Missouri State Archives and the St. Louis Genealogical Society.

Deeds

Deeds are the beginning point in your search for records, as they will tell you the names of the previous owners as well as provide clues as to what may have been located on the property at the time the deed was drawn up. The conveyance of land between two or more individuals is documented by the recording of a deed. A deed tells you the grantor (seller) and the grantee (buyer) of the property, lists the purchase price, provides a legal description, and may say whether there was a mortgage. It also may mention the existence of the house and additions to it. A sharp increase in the purchase price may indicate that a building was added to the property. Pay special attention to the legal description in each deed you come across to make certain you are still looking at the correct property. Just because the name you are researching is listed doesn't mean it is necessarily your property. Make sure that each legal description matches yours.

There will be two dates listed on each deed – the date the deed was signed, and the date the deed was recorded. You are interested in the date the deed was signed, as this is when the property actually changed hands. The date the deed was recorded can be weeks or months after the deed was actually signed.

- ### *Grantors and Grantees*

Before beginning your search through the deeds, you will need to be familiar with two terms – grantor and grantee. The grantor is the seller of the property, and is usually listed first. The grantee is the buyer. If you look at your own deed, you will be listed as the grantee and the person you bought the house from will be shown as the grantor. Sometimes, the previous deed will be mentioned in the present deed, and you can see when the current grantor was a grantee. If not, you will need to look up the current grantor in the Grantee Indexes. In fact, it is advisable to look for all of the property owners in both indexes, because sometimes the property transaction only appears in one of the indexes. This is the method you will use to work your way back through the owners of the property. Included in Appendix II on pages 52-53 are St. Louis County Deeds Research Logs for you to write down each grantor and grantee, along with the dates and page citations. I made photo-

copies of each deed I came across because I found it interesting
to read the different descriptions of the property and because
sometimes the instrument was not just listed as a deed but
was noted as something else. For example, if you come across
a Deed of Trust, it generally does not mean that the property
changed hands, but instead the grantor gives title of the property to a grantee (usually the person lending the money) until
the grantor pays the loan back in full. It is not necessary to
make the copies, but do note anything different about the deed
on your worksheets.

*This general warranty deed shows the grantor and grantee,
and provides a legal description of the property.*

- ***Look at Surrounding Deeds***

As you come across deeds on the property, check the deeds that were recorded on the pages immediately before and after your deed. You might find other deeds relating to your property. A caution: Remember that while the deeds will tell you who owned the property, they won't tell you who lived there. You will need to look at the other records listed later in this book to determine who actually occupied the house.

- ***Court References***

If you come across any references to court cases within the deeds, make note of them on the Abstract of Deed form located in Appendix II on pages 54-55 as they might contain useful information about the house or its owners. Ask the staff person in the Recorder of Deeds office where you might locate the court records.

- ***Accessing the Deeds***

Now, let's walk through how you actually access the deeds. When you first enter the Recorder of Deeds office, approach the Deed Copies counter on your right hand side and ask for assistance. The clerk will look up the address on the department computer, which covers deeds back to 1973, and will print a copy of what is obtained.

Then the clerk will look up the address on a School Tape, which will take the property back to the 1940s, 1950s or 1960s, depending on the property. Once you get the oldest Grantee off of this file, you will be taken to a computer to look through the Inverted Files, which date back to 1877. The Inverted Files are alphabetical by grantee name, but only as to the first letter of the last name. For example, when I was looking for Emmett

Deed Search Results

Please note that The Recorder of Deeds Office provides several services which allow you to search for deed records from the comfort of your home or office. For more information please visit the Deed Search Remote Access page.

7 Records Found   Page 1 of 1

Search By: Locator Number

Search Criteria: Locator Number: 22J131772

Line Number	Grantor Name	Grantee Name	Date, Document Number	Affected Book, Page	Book, Page	Locator - Lien Number	Instrument Type	Legal Description
1		Mueller Georgia L *et al*	00/00/0000 0		7738 107	22J131772 -	UNKWN	
2	Davis Richard L & Lynn...	Mueller Georgia L *et al*, Swyres Rocky R & Janic...	04/09/1985 669		7738 107	22J131772 -	WD	Shrewsbury Park 1St Sub Lot 12 Blk 3
3	Mueller Georgia L Now ..., Swyres Janice L *et al*, Wright Georgia L & Jam...	Bearden D Keith & Elle...	12/20/1991 485		9166 1907	22J131772 -	WD	Shrewsbury Park 1St Sub Lto 12 Blk 3
4	Bearden D Keith By*tr*..., Bearden Ellen C By*tr*..., Goldfarb Milton P*trE*..., Nationsbank By*tret al*	S And P Properties Inc	09/19/1997 407	10288 874	11295 1161	22J131772 -	TRS-D	Shrewsbury Park 1 Lot 12 Blk 3 Pb 3 Pg 7
5	S And P Properties	G Stafford Co	04/13/1998 1110		11548 1348	22J131772 -	QCD	Shrewsbury Park 1 Lot 12 Blk 3 Pb 3 Pg 7
6	G Stafford Co	W L S 7722 L L C	08/12/1998 1042		11719 2171	22J131772 -	WD	Shrewsbury Park 1 Lot 12 Blk 3 Pb 3 Pg 7
7	W L S 7722 L L C	Pioneer Bank And Trust...	08/12/1998 1044		11719 2182	22J131772 -	ESMT	Shrewsbury Park 1 Lot 12 Blk 3 Pb 3 Pg 7

Note that recording of locator numbers is not a requirement. Therefore be aware that locator number searches may not produce thorough search results, as locator numbers are not always recorded.

This page shows recorded deed index information for the indicated locator number.

Deed documents are not available online but are available at the public terminals in the Recorder of Deeds office. Deed documents may also be obtained by mailing the completed Deed Copy Order Form (PDF) to the Recorders of Deeds office with appropriate fees.

Using the deed search at the Recorder of Deeds office will give you a head start on who owned the property.

Fitzgerald, one of the property owners of a house I was researching in Shrewsbury, I had to scroll through ALL of the last names beginning with "F." Sometimes the handwritten entries are illegible. Scan each page for the property's legal description as well. If you have no other clues as to the date, you will have to look through each year in the index. This can be very time consuming.

Fortunately for my search, I had discovered through City Directories that Emmett Fitzgerald lived at the address I was researching all the way back to 1938. So, I began to look for him as a grantee in 1937 and worked my way back from that date. That one piece of information saved me looking through fifty years of Inverted Files. See the section on City Directories later in this book for more information on how these valuable resources can aid your research.

Once you locate your grantee and determine that the legal description of the property is the correct one, write down the date, book and page number of the deed. You will then pull the film containing that book number from the large vertical storage areas and read it on a microfilm reader. The grantor listed on the deed is the next grantee you will look up in the Inverted Files. These microfilm readers will print copies as well.

If you choose not to make copies, make sure that you at least fill in the pertinent information on the St. Louis County Deeds Research Log, noting the source of the information. You can also use the Abstract of Deed form located in Appendix II on pages 54-55 if you need more room to write. If you do want to make copies while at the deed's office, request the copy directly from the microfilm reader. There is no need to insert any money. Look at each page carefully to be sure the entire page copied and is legible. When you are through with your research for the day, simply take your copies to the staff person at the Deeds Copies counter, who will make up a ticket for you. Take the ticket to the cashier's office, located in the same room, to pay for your copies.

• *Creating a Property Timeline*

Using the grantee and grantor logs you completed from your deed research, make a list of all the families who owned your property on the Property Timeline included in Appendix II on pages 56-57. This sheet will be a handy reference of names and time periods as you search through other records to learn about your family or families.

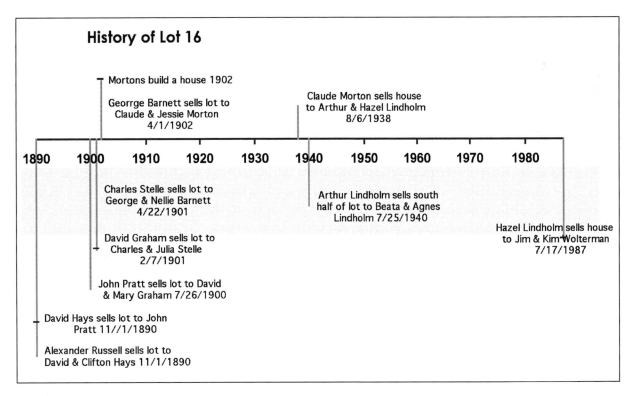

A property timeline laid out in a horizontal format makes it easy to see when the property changed hands.

• *Plat Maps*

While you are at the county government center, stop and take a look at the subdivision plat maps in the Recorder of Deeds office. You can see how the neighborhood was laid out. A plat map is a plan of an area that shows the boundaries of various subdivisions. Recorded with the county at the time a neighborhood is developed, it will show a plan of the streets, and indicate any existing structures. It will also list the owners of the land that made up that particular plat. There will be plat maps from previous years, as well as the current year, so you can look for changes in ownership on the maps. It is also fun to look at the properties surrounding the one you are researching. For individual property plats, go to the Assessors Office on the 3rd floor.

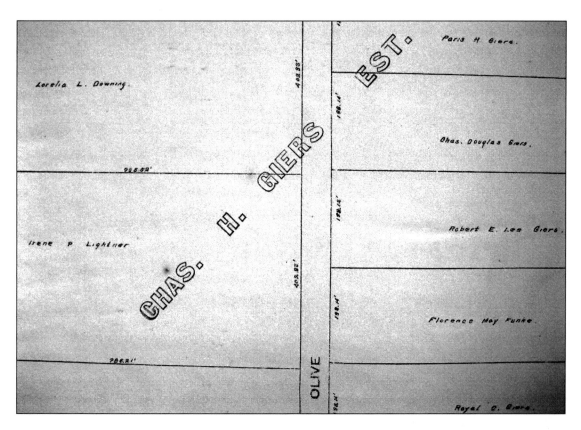

This 1909 county plat map shows the property owners on Olive.

• *More Than You Bargained For?*

Now, if all of this seems overwhelming to you, or you are just
not interested in doing the research yourself, you can have a
Title Insurance Company obtain a chain of title for you. There
will be a fee charged for the service, but if you provide the
company with a legal description of your property the work
can be done for you.

Key

*The St. Louis County Library has available on microfilm St. Louis
City deed records through Volume R (1832) and St. Louis County
deed records from Book 1 (1877) through Book 1128 (September
1931) in the Special Collections Department.*

Real Estate Tax Records

Okay. So, you have deeds to the property and possibly now
know the names of everyone who bought or sold the land. (If
you don't have all the names but instead hit a roadblock, take
heart. Some of the other resources in this book may help you
find answers.) The problem is you still can't tell when the
house was built. You might find the answer in the tax records.
St. Louis County real estate tax records only go back twenty-
five years. But you might find some other tax records through
your local municipality. For example, the City of Webster
Groves incorporated in 1896 and tax records exist from that
year forward.

Real estate tax records will list the person paying the taxes
each year, and this is usually the property owner. Keep in mind
that when you look at real estate tax records, the taxes for any
given year reflect the value of the property in the preceding

year. So the Webster Groves record of taxes collected in 1897 represents taxes on the property in 1896. What you are looking for in these records is a significant jump in property taxes from one year to the next. This will be a clue that a building or an addition was constructed on the property. You will want additional documentation of the exact year, though, as it may have taken the assessor's office a while to catch up with the new construction.

Key

Check with your local municipality, library and historical society for any tax records.

Building Permits

The most definitive evidence of the construction of a house is a building permit, which is a document that grants permission to construct or make renovations to a building. Sometimes the building permit will even list the name of the architect. St. Louis County only has building permits for the past ten years. Your best bet will be to contact your local municipality to see if they have maintained the building permits for your community. Even if your house was built before building permits were kept, you may still find information about later modifications and additions to your house.

If you do locate a building permit, note the name of the homeowner and any architect involved. While you are at your local municipal office, ask about the existence of any separate files for acquisitions of city easements, installation of sewers, and other city activities.

Key

Check with your local municipality for any building permit records.

Maps and Atlases

Atlases and maps provide a visual history of an area. While a map is usually just one sheet of paper, an atlas is generally a bound collection of maps, charts, plates or tables. Historical city and county maps and atlases may show your home on them, and perhaps even list the owner's name as well. These maps often show the location of roads and other landmarks that may no longer exist. Julius Pitzman was an early St. Louis County surveyor, and his 1868 map is a detailed accounting of St. Louis City and County prior to the separation. An atlas was completed by Pitzman in 1878. There are other local atlases available as well.

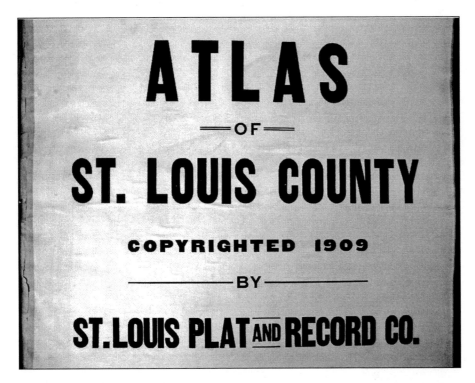

Atlases may indicate your property owner.

• *Plat Maps*

As mentioned earlier, a plat map is a plan of an area which shows the legal boundaries and dimensions of each parcel of land. These maps can be found at the St. Louis County Government Center. Check for the property owners of your parcel of land on each of the plat maps you locate.

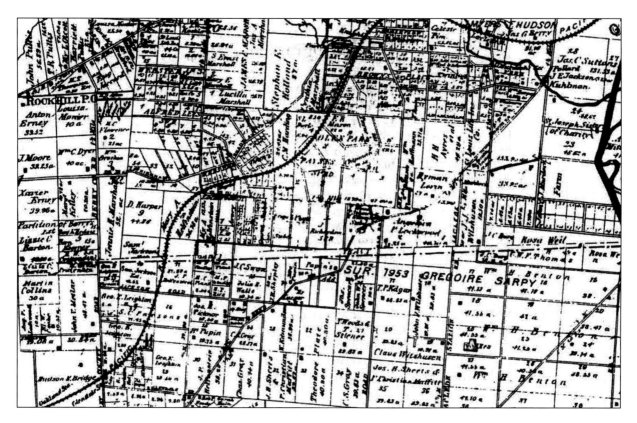

1868 plat map.

- *Fire Insurance Maps*

During the late nineteenth and early twentieth centuries, fire insurance maps were periodically drawn up for cities and towns in the United States. These maps were commissioned by insurance companies in order to more accurately calculate fire risk, depicting the layout of the town and showing each existing building. The maps offer a great deal of information, and can show the outline of the building, the building material, the number of stories, doors, windows and chimneys, the address and lot lines, street widths, water pipes, hydrants and cisterns. The Sanborn Company was the largest, but not the only, fire insurance mapping firm. The Sanborn Company was founded in 1867, and created fire insurance maps from 1867 until 1969.

For St. Louis County, the earliest Sanborn map is from 1909. Some libraries carry the Sanborn maps on microfilm. Look up your property on the various maps and check for any existing house and outbuildings, such as a garage, shed or barn. The house number will be located at the front edge of the lot. Make note of the number as it was not unusual for the house number, or even street name, to change over the years. If you can find your property on a succession of maps, you can see how it changed over time.

The fire insurance maps were updated somewhat irregularly, based upon the likelihood that enough had changed to make possible the sale of updated maps. However, when found, they can offer proof of the existence of your home and represent a unique snapshot of the community.

Key

Whenever you are at a library, government center or historical society, ask about the maps and atlases in their collections. The Missouri History Museum Library and Research Center in St. Louis holds several atlases of St. Louis County that show the names of landowners, particularly for the nineteenth and early twentieth centuries, as well as a collection of Sanborn and Whipple fire insurance maps. The University of Missouri has digitized some of their collection of Sanborn fire insurance maps, and they can be found online at http://digital.library.umsystem.edu/cgi/i/ image/image-idx?page=index;c=umcscsanic. The St. Louis County Library subscribes to the Digital Sanborn Maps database. It can be found at http://www.slcl.org/databases/atoz.htm#S, and can be accessed at the library itself or from any computer if you have a current St. Louis County Library card.

Newspapers

Local newspapers can offer a wealth of information, and many are available on microfilm or microfiche. In looking up each of the property owners in the newspapers you might first of all find some obituaries. The obituaries in the late 1800s and early 1900s often provided information on when the person moved to town, the occupation, and the names of parents, spouses and children. It is becoming more common to find obituary indexes for local newspapers. Once you have obtained the death dates of your previous property owners, the best way to find the obituary is to look in the newspaper for the first few days following the individual's death.

Newspapers also can provide social highlights about family members as well as coverage of local affairs in the city and county. When you find the year that the house was built, looking through newspapers from that time period will give you a sense of what life was like in St. Louis County. Various newspapers in the past also reported construction news based on information received from building permit applications.

Key

Your local library, the St. Louis County Library, the St. Louis Genealogical Society and the Missouri History Museum Library and Research Center in St. Louis all have newspaper collections available for research. The St. Louis County Library has microfilm of the St. Louis County Watchman-Advocate, *which was published in Clayton and focused specifically on the county. The library has begun to index this newspaper, and you can access it at http://www.slcl.org/ branches/hq/sc/indexes/watchman/watchmanindexmain.htm. The St. Louis Public Library's online St. Louis Obituary Index http://www.slpl.org/slpl/ gateways/article240117800.asp is also a good source. Additionally, the Missouri History Museum Library and Research Center in St. Louis holds a collection of Necrology Scrapbooks that contains photocopies of death notices, obituaries, and probate announcements clipped from St. Louis newspapers circa 1880s-1970s. These scrapbooks don't contain every obituary from every local newspaper for this period, but they are worth reviewing. The St. Louis Mercantile Library's website http://www.umsl.edu/mercantile/special_ collections/slma-112.html has a searchable database of articles from the* St. Louis Globe Democrat.

Joseph Kubler Drops Dead.

Joseph Kubler, a prominent citizen of this place, dropped dead last Sunday morning, at St. Gabriel's church, of heart disease, to which he was subject. Before and after going to church that morning, the deceased appeared to be in the best of health and spirits, and his sudden death was a shock to the whole community.

The deceased was born in Buserach Canton Solotum, Switzerland, February 14, 1850, and emigrated to this country two years later, landing in New Orleans. From there he came to Cincinnati where he lived until 1866, when he went to Louisville, Kentucky, and was married to Josephine Hildebrand in 1867. In 1871 he moved to Memphis, Tennessee, from which place he came to Indiana, locating in Indianapolis. In 1877, he with his family, moved to this city where he resided until his death. He was a wood carver by trade and is said to have been very proficient in his profession. He started a grocery store on South Central Avenue where he carried on business about two years, when he sold out to Adam Frank. Mr. Kubler was a man of many good qualities, always kind and agreeable to his neighbors. He was a kind husband and father, and leaves three sons and a loving wife who will miss his counsel and companionship. The remains of the deceased was interred from the Catholic church yesterday morning at 9 o'clock, Father Rudolf officiating, followed by a large concourse of relatives and friends. The widow and children have the sympathy of the entire community. Deceased was thirty-six years, seven months and five days old at the time of his death.

An obituary from 1886 provides a lot of personal history about the deceased.

City Directories

City directories were the forerunners to telephone books as they were published prior to the invention of the telephone. Like phone books, the city directories list residents' names, dwellings, and businesses. However they provide additional information that phone books do not. Directories often listed the resident's occupation and spouse in addition to the address. An entry for a widow sometimes listed her deceased spouse's name as well.

The directories can help you establish the dates that a person lived at a specific address. The names are listed in alphabetical order. St. Louis City directories were first published in 1821, and did not come out on a regular basis until 1865. Some St. Louis County residents will be included in the City directories. St. Louis County directories first appeared in 1893, were not published every year, and ended publication in 1979.

You can also utilize the reverse directories, located in the back of the city directories beginning in 1922. These are arranged by address, not name. Once you locate the address in the reverse directory, you can see who lived at the house. Look up the new name in the front of the directory for additional information on the occupant.

If the person who lived in the home was a business owner, also check the business section of directories to see if the business was operated out of the home. Having the name of the business enables you to look for additional information in business directories and other biographical sources. Keep in mind that a period of time passed between the compilation of the information for the directory and the actual publication date. Use the

An early St. Louis County Directory, listing the residents of the county and their occupations.

Jackson Ruben, Laborer, Eddie & Park Rd............Jennings
Jackson S, Gardener, Redman Av...............Sappington
Jackson Sam, Farmer, Spoede Av.............Black Jack
Jackson S R, Merchant, Cherry Av.............Stratman
*Jackson Walter, Farmer, R. Henry Jackson, Hog Hollow Rd, Lake
Jackson Wm S, Farmer, Marshall Av...............Tuxedo
*Jacob Barney, Laborer, R. Fred Schwaaf Jr, Lemay Rd..Mattese
Jacob Charles, Laborer, Eatherton Rd...............Grover
Jacob Edward, Farmer, Valley Rd...............Ellisville
Jacob Hy, Sen., Farmer, Valley Rd...............Ellisville
Jacob Hy, Jr., Farmer, Valley Rd...............Ellisville
Jacob Martin, Farmer, Natural Bridge Rd.............Bridgeton
Jacob Michael, Gardener, Weil Av...............Old Orchard
Jacobe Hugo S, Town Recorder, Madison Av.............Kirkwood
*Jacobs Mrs A H, Swan Av...............Webster
Jacobs George, Farmer, Manchester Rd.............Ellisville
Jacobs Henry, Laborer...............Fenton
Central

Entries in the 1896 St. Louis County Directory.

City Directory Log in Appendix II on pages 58-59 to help keep track of the directories you have researched. A caution: Remember that while the directories will tell you where a person lived, that doesn't mean the person owned the property. Use the other records mentioned in this book to determine ownership.

Key

Your local library, the St. Louis County Library, the St. Louis Genealogical Society and the Missouri History Museum Library and Research Center in St. Louis all have city and county directories available for research.

Photographs

In addition to photographs you may have already secured, many local museums, libraries, and historical associations maintain photograph files. While you are visiting the local repositories, be sure to inquire about any photos they may have on file. You may not come across photos of your own home, but you may find others from your community. These will enhance your visualization of what things looked like when your home-owners or ancestors lived in the area.

The Mortons enjoy a tea party in the backyard of their Webster Groves home.

Key

Whenever you are at a library, research center or historical society, ask about the photographs held in their collections.

Vital Records

Vital records are the records of life events that are kept under governmental authority. Examples include birth certificates, marriage licenses, divorce records, and death certificates. These documents can reveal quite a bit about your grantors and grantees, such as when they were born or died, to whom they were married, and the names of their parents. Record all the information you find, as it may come in handy later in your research. If the previous owners are deceased, you may want to request the death certificate to identify approximate dates when the property could have changed hands.

Key

The St. Louis County Recorder of Deeds Office has records of marriages and probate records from 1877 to the present, and county court records from 1877 to the present, including probate, divorce and naturalization records. Civil and criminal court cases are in the St. Louis County Circuit Clerks Office, and the St. Louis County Office of Vital Statistics has records of births and deaths since 1883. Additionally, the St. Louis County Library has birth, marriage, death, funeral home, cemetery and church records available for research. The Missouri State Archives Death Certificate Database (starting in 1910) is available at http://www.sos. mo.gov/archives/resources/deathcertificates/ for online searches.

Last Will and Testaments

If you have a break in your chain of title, it could be because ownership of the property transferred by inheritance rather than by sale. Wills can provide access to this type of transfer, and they are found with probate records. Probate records, which are court proceedings to pass a deceased person's property to the heirs, are located in the county clerk's office. Wills are a matter of public record and provide a great deal of information, and usually include who inherited the house. When looking at wills, there are two terms you need to know. The devisor is the party who grants property by bequest or will. The devisee is the party who receives property by bequest or will.

With your list of grantors and grantees in hand, see if any of the names appear in either the devisor or devisee indexes. Wills are usually indexed by last name. If you find one of your names, request a copy of the will to review. Write down all the pertinent information on the Abstract of Will form, which can be found in Appendix II on pages 60-61, including the date when the will was probated. This will give you the approximate date of death of the devisor. You will also want to write down all the heirs in the will, as they or their descendants may still be in the area and available for interviewing. An added bonus of looking at wills is that you may find a list of personal belongings which passed with the house. With the approximate date of death now in hand, you can conduct a search for an obituary in the local newspapers.

 Key

St. Louis County Library has probate records available in the Special Collections department, and the Missouri History Museum Library and Research Center in St. Louis has some

indexes to probate records. The Missouri State Archives has digi-
tized the 19th century St. Louis probate records, and they can be
found at http://www.sos.mo.gov/archives/mojudicial/default.asp

Court Records

The St. Louis County Clerk of Court's Office is located in the
St. Louis County Courthouse, 7900 Carondelet, Clayton,
Missouri. When looking at court records, there are two additional words with which you need to be familiar. A plaintiff
is the party who institutes a suit in court. A defendant is
the party against whom an action is brought. Go through the
plaintiff and defendant indexes, looking for the names of your
grantors and grantees. If you find any matches, copy down the
reference number, and ask the person at the desk to bring you
the appropriate court records. You might find interesting information about the house or its owners in a court case.

Key

County court records are also available at the St. Louis County
Library in the Special Collections department.

Census Records

Through census records you can discover the names of everyone who lived in the house you are researching, as well as their
relationship to each other. Federal census reports came out
every 10 years, beginning in 1830 for Missouri. Due to privacy
issues, the most recent census available to the public is 1930.
(The 1940 census will become available in 2012.) These records
not only show where a family lived in a given census year, but
also the age, gender, marital status, place of birth and occupa-

1920 Census record

tions of each household member. The house number and street name are listed on some census schedules. Check the various census years. Because the census taker went door to door down a street, you can see who the neighbors were as well. Indexes of the various censuses have been published because the census records themselves are not listed alphabetically. Instead, they are in the order in which each house was visited by the census taker. Remember that just because a person lived in a house does not mean that he or she owned it, but it is another path for you to follow. Blank census forms are available in Appendix II on pages 62-71. Note that the 1890 Missouri Federal census was destroyed by a fire.

Key

Census records for St. Louis City and County are available on micro-film at the St. Louis County Library and the Missouri History Museum Library and Research Center in St. Louis. You can also access these records online through various subscription services. The St. Louis County Library subscribes to HeritageQuest and Ancestry.com, and you can review the census records at a library location.

Biographical Sources

Biographical information on your property owners may be found in a variety of sources, such as newspaper articles, diaries, organization rosters, and school directories. Many times when organizations, towns, or counties published their histories, they included biographical sketches of members or citizens. I found my homeowner, Claude Morton, in one such publication; and, from there, I learned that he was active in Webster Groves politics, the local library, and First Congregational Church. This small biography led me to several more sources to look for information about him and his family.

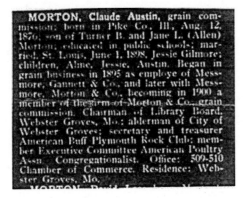

Biographical sketch of Claude Morton.

Key

Your local library and historical society, the St. Louis County Library, the St. Louis Genealogical Society and the Missouri History Museum Library and Research Center in St. Louis may all have books containing biographical sketches. Further, the Missouri History Museum Library and Research Center has a searchable Genealogy and Local History Index available at http://www.mohistory.org/genealogy. While you are at their website, check out their new street address search at http://www.mohistory.org/genealogy/addresses. You can enter the house or building address you are researching to see what references to it exist at this library. If you don't get a hit on your exact house number, try entering the first number of your address followed by asterisks for the remaining numbers, then the street address. For example, my address of 213 South Maple yielded no results, but when I entered 2** South Maple, I found two biographical sketch references to men who lived at addresses near my house in the past.

Family Histories

Published family histories can provide a wealth of information about your grantors and grantees. The Family History Library in Salt Lake City has more than 70,000 biography and family history volumes. You can search names online at http://www.familysearch.org, or visit one of the local Family History Libraries located at 10445 Clayton Road in Frontenac or 6386 Howdershell in Hazelwood.

Key

Check with your local library and historical society, the St. Louis County Library, the St. Louis Genealogical Society and the Missouri History Museum Library and Research Center in St. Louis for family histories.

Local Histories

During the late 1800s, large numbers of city and county histories were commissioned. The St. Louis area was no exception. While providing a great deal of information regarding the development of the town or county, these histories often offered detailed information about the residents who resided there. Many contain early photographs of the people and community as well, including homes and businesses. You can look in the indexes of these histories for all of the names of your homeowners or ancestors.

Key

Check with your local library and historical society, the St. Louis County Library, the St. Louis Genealogical Society, and the Missouri History Museum Library and Research Center in St. Louis for any local histories in their collections.

JOSEPH KUBLER,
GROCERIES AND PROVISIONS.

Eligibly and centrally located at the corner of Central Avenue and First St., occupying a sales-room 18x40 feet in size, with a basement of corresponding dimensions, is the popular family grocery and provision store of Mr. Joseph Kubler, which although established as recently as 1883, has already secured a trade entitling it to a prominent rank among its older contemporaries. The stock carried by Mr. Kubler, which is fresh and desirable, is selected with an especial view to the requirements of his trade and comprises a general line of choice family groceries and provisions, teas, coffees, spices, sugars, syrups, foreign and domestic fruits, tobacco and cigars, canned goods and miscellaneous merchandise pertaining to this special branch of trade. The stock is daily replenished by fresh arrivals from importers, jobbers, manufacturers and producers, and the prices are uniformly the lowest consistent with the quality of the goods offered. The trade of this house, which is derived from both city and country, has steadily increased since its inception, and each succeeding month witnesses a most gratifying increase of business. Mr. Kubler, who is a native of Switzerland, was born in 1850, and came to this country when but four years of age. He first engaged in business on his own account in this city, and by a strict adherence to the correct principles of mercantile honor and fair and honorable dealing, has built up his present prosperous and lucrative business, and earned an enviable reputation as a conscientious and upright merchant, whose representations will always be found to accord strictly with the facts.

A county history relays a great amount of information about one of its local businessmen.

Land Grants

Missouri's earliest land records are those from the French and Spanish governments because at various times between the 1680s and early 1800s, these two governments controlled the land from which the state of Missouri would later be created. During that time, land grants were issued to settlers in the area. If your property dates back to this period, then you will be looking for the actual grants of land from the French and Spanish governments to your grantee.

Some later settlers who came to Missouri purchased land from the United States government. This conveyance was through the issuance of a land patent by the federal government. However, in the 1800s the federal government donated 6.5 million acres of land to the state of Missouri, which in turn sold off the land. The state issued land patents, which contained the name of the person who purchased the land, the purchase and patent dates, and a legal description of the property.

 ## Key

The Missouri History Museum Library and Research Center in St. Louis holds a variety of colonial and 19th century Missouri land records. Many of the land patents issued between 1820 and 1908 are available in digitized format from the Bureau of Land Management website at http://www.glorecords.blm.gov. The Missouri State Archives also hold records of the public domain land given to the state by the federal government upon statehood. The Missouri Land Patent database contains over 35,000 transcribed land patents. Go to http://www.sos.mo.gov/archives/land/ to search their database online.

Architectural Collections

You will need to know the name of the architect who built your house in order for these records to be of any benefit to you. Most homes were not designed by an architect, but instead were built by plans purchased by the builder. However, if you do know which architect was involved in the building of your home, these collections can be both interesting and informative.

Key

*The Missouri History Museum Library and Research Center in
St. Louis has a fairly extensive architecture collection.*

The Internet

The Internet has changed forever how we access data and per-
form research. In fact, the Internet helped me find the building date of my house. Putting my genealogical skills to work,
I entered the name of the individual on the oldest deed I had
located, Claude Morton, into a search engine. Lo and behold, I
found a reference to him in a family tree put on the Internet by
his great-granddaughter, Holly Burt. I emailed Holly through
the contact information she had listed, and she sent me some
pictures of houses she had in a box given to her by her grandmother. Three of the photos were of my house. Eventually,
I traveled to Holly's home, and together, we poured through
scrapbooks put together by her grandmother. A fascinating
picture of early Webster Groves emerged from her collection.
But most important for me, Holly's grandmother had typed the
obituary for her father, Claude, upon his death. In it she stated
that "the Mortons lived for 36 years at the home they had built
at 213 S. Maple Avenue in Webster Groves." It just doesn't get
any better than that!

Many organizations are creating online catalogs of their hold-
ings. Be sure to check the websites mentioned in this book, as
well as others suggested to you, as new information is being
added on a daily basis. Enter the names of all of your grantees

and grantors into the search engines. You never know what might pop up on any of them. Document your web visits on the Research Log. As you locate books and records that may be helpful to you in your research, you can add them to your Research To-Do List so that when you visit the library or other repository you can go right to the reference. This will save you valuable research time.

Section Three: Putting It All Together

Your House Story

You have completed your research. Congratulations! You now have a binder filled with the chronological history of your house, or the house of your ancestor, and its previous owners. You have obtained your century home plaque, your historic designation, records of renovations, or perhaps the location of the family homestead you were looking for in your search. What now?

What happens next is up to you. Perhaps you have accomplished all you set out to do, and your binder will go in a drawer or on a shelf. If so, that's fine. But if you are like I am, your historical appetite has now been whetted. After all the effort, energy and time this project has consumed, you want to share what you have learned. You want to make your house and its families come to life. It's time to write the house history!

By the time I ultimately discovered the first owner of my house my genealogy chromosome had kicked in, and I felt like the Mortons were part of my extended family. I knew where the family worshipped, what Claude Morton did for a living, what organizations he was active in, and where the children went to

Jessie and Aline Morton

school. I also had photographs of the family and the house and had met a descendant of the original owners of the house. I could not just leave this family on my bookshelf. I wrote about my research experience and my "family", and submitted it to my local historical society and local newspaper. My "family" wasn't one of the founding families of Webster Groves, so it had not been published in any of the books written about my community. Nor had my house appeared in any publication previously. Just as every person has a story to tell, so does every house. And who better to tell it than **me** – the person who spent three years to get to the bottom of the mystery!

Your house story can be as simple or involved as you would like to make it. There are no rules – yea! – as you are writing this just to please yourself. The goal is to create a complete picture of the lives of the people living in your house at a particular time. You can create a timeline of your home's past and use it to write a narrative. Discussions of why the family moved to the house, what the neighborhood was like, and what was going on in the community at that time are some topics to cover. The addition of photographs, family quotes, or copies of vital records are certainly pertinent as well, and add dimension to the story.

The use of sources such as *Historic Preservation, American Heritage* and *Old House Journal* can help you understand the social and historic aspects of each time period you are researching, and add depth to your descriptions of the past events. A review of old cookbooks, women's magazines, and advertisements can also assist you in reconstructing the daily lives of previous property owners.

As you are part of your home's history, be sure to include information and pictures of any changes you have made to the house. When complete, your house story can be submitted to the local historical society, library, historical magazines, or genealogical websites so that your home will have a place in history. Future homeowners and genealogists who research their ancestors will thank you for bringing this past history into the present.

Appendix I. Resources

Missouri State Archives
Secretary of State
Records Management and Archives Division
600 West Main Street
Jefferson City, MO 65102
573-751-3280
www.sos.mo.gov/archives

State Historical Society of Missouri
1020 Lowry Street
Columbia, MO 65201-7207
800-747-6366
http://shs.umsystem.edu/index.shtml

St. Louis County Recorder of Deeds Division
Lawrence K. Roos County Government Building
41 S. Central Avenue, 4th Floor
Clayton, MO 63105
314-615-2500
http://revenue.stlouisco.com/RecorderOfDeeds

Recorder of Deeds
St. Louis City Hall
1200 Market Street, Room 126
St. Louis, MO 63103-2881
314-622-4610
http://stlouis.missouri.org/citygov/recorder

St. Louis County Library
1640 S. Lindbergh Blvd.
St. Louis, MO 63131
314- 994-3300
www.slcl.org

Family History Library
10445 Clayton Road
St. Louis, MO 63131-2909
314-993-2328

Family History Library
6386 Howdershell Rd.
Hazelwood, MO 63042-1122
314-731-5373

St. Louis Genealogical Society
#4 Sunnen Drive, Suite 140
St. Louis, MO 63143
314-647-8547
www.stlgs.org

Missouri History Museum
Library and Research Center
225 South Skinker
St. Louis, MO 63105-2317
www.mohistory.org/lrc-home

Mailing Address Only:
Missouri History Museum
Library and Research Center
P.O. Box 11940
St. Louis, MO 63112-0040

continued next page

Circuit Court of St. Louis County
7900 Carondelet Avenue
Clayton, MO 63105
314-615-8029
www.co.st-louis.mo.us/circuitcourt

St. Louis County Vital Statistics
111 South Meramec Avenue, 1st Floor
St. Louis, MO 63105-1711
314-615-0376
www.co.st-louis.mo.us/doh/vitals/vitals.html

St. Louis Mercantile Library
Thomas Jefferson Library Building
One University Blvd.
St. Louis, Missouri 63121-4400
314-516-7240
http://www.umsl.edu/mercantile/index.html

Appendix II. Forms

Research Log

Date of Search	Location/ Call No./URL	Facility or Website Visited	Description of Source (author, title, year, pages)	Comments

Research Log

Date of Search	Location/ Call No./URL	Facility or Website Visited	Description of Source (author, title, year, pages)	Comments

Correspondence Log

Date Sent	Adressee/Postal Address or Email Address	Record/Information Requested	Money Sent	Date Replied	Results

Correspondence Log

Date Sent	Adressee/Postal Address or Email Address	Record/Information Requested	Money Sent	Date Replied	Results

Research To-Do List

Item/ Information Needed	Location Where Item/ Information Can Be Found	Comments

Research To-Do List

Item/ Information Needed	Location Where Item/ Information Can Be Found	Comments

St. Louis County Deeds Research Log

Date of Instrument	Date of Filing	Grantor (Seller)	Grantee (Buyer)	Description of Property	Type of Deed	Book	Page No.

St. Louis County Deeds Research Log

Date of Instrument	Date of Filing	Grantor (Seller)	Grantee (Buyer)	Description of Property	Type of Deed	Book	Page No.

Abstract of Deed

Deed Book:	
Page Number:	
Type of Deed:	
Date of Instrument:	Date of Filing:
Grantor:	
Amount of Money Paid:	
Legal Description of Property:	
Other Items of Interest Mentioned:	

Abstract of Deed

Deed Book:	
Page Number:	
Type of Deed:	
Date of Instrument:	Date of Filing:
Grantor:	
Amount of Money Paid:	
Legal Description of Property:	
Other Items of Interest Mentioned:	

Property Timeline

Year	Owner	Description

Property Timeline

Year	Owner	Description

City Directory Log

Directory Name	Year	Page	Name	Address	Occupation/Business Address	Notes

City Directory Log

Directory Name	Year	Page	Name	Address	Occupation/Business Address	Notes

Abstract of Will

County:	Source:	Page Number:	Date and Place of Will:	Date and Place Probated:	Name of Person Making the Will:	Residence:	Bequests:	Name of Executor:	Witnesses:

Abstract of Will

County:										
Source:										
Page Number:										
Date and Place of Will:										
Date and Place Probated:										
Name of Person Making the Will:										
Residence:										
Bequests:										
Name of Executor:										
Witnesses:										

1880 U.S. Federal Census

State:

County:

City:

Page:

Enumeration District:

Call #/URL:

Enumeration Date:

										Name of Street	
										House Number	
									1	Dwelling Number	
									2	Family Number	
									3	Name of each person whose place of abode on June 1, 1880 was in this family.	
									4	Color	
									5	Sex	
									6	Age	
									7	Month born if during census year	
									8	Relationship to head of household	
									9	Single	
									10	Married	
									11	Widowed/Divorced	
									12	Married during this year	
									13	Profession, occupation or trade	
									14	Months unemployed this year	
									15	Currently sick? Specify.	
									16	Blind	
									17	Deaf & dumb	
									18	Idiotic	
									19	Insane	
									20	Disabled	
									21	Attended school this year	
									22	Cannot read	
									23	Cannot write	
									24	Birthplace of this person	
									25	Birthplace of father	
									26	Birthplace of mother	

1880 U.S. Federal Census

State:

County:

City:

Page:

Enumeration District:

Call #/URL:

Enumeration Date:

									Name of Street
									House Number
								1	Dwelling Number
								2	Family Number
								3	Name of each person whose place of abode on June 1, 1880 was in this family.
								4	Color
								5	Sex
								6	Age
								7	Month born if during census year
								8	Relationship to head of household
								9	Single
								10	Married
								11	Widowed/Divorced
								12	Married during this year
								13	Profession, occupation or trade
								14	Months unemployed this year
								15	Currently sick? Specify.
								16	Blind
								17	Deaf & dumb
								18	Idiotic
								19	Insane
								20	Disabled
								21	Attended school this year
								22	Cannot read
								23	Cannot write
								24	Birthplace of this person
								25	Birthplace of father
								26	Birthplace of mother

										Name of Street
										House Number
									1	Dwelling Number
									2	Family Number
									3	Name of each person whose place of abode on June 1, 1900 was in this family.
									4	Relationship to head of household
									5	Color
									6	Sex
									7	Month and year of birth
									8	Age at last birthday
									9	Single, widowed, married, divorced
									10	# of years married
									11	Mother of how many children
									12	# of children living
									13	Birthplace of this person
									14	Birthplace of father
									15	Birthplace of mother
									16	Year of immigration
									17	# years in the US
									18	Naturalized citizen
									19	Occupation of everyone over 10 years
									20	# months not employed
									21	# months attended school this year
									22	Can read
									23	Can write
									24	Speaks English
									25	Owned or rented
									26	Owned free or mortgaged
									27	Farm or house
									28	No. of farm schedule

1900 U.S. Federal Census

State:

County:

City:

Page:

Enumeration District:

Call #/URL:

Enumeration Date:

1900 U.S. Federal Census

State:

County:

City:

Page:

Enumeration District:

Call #/URL:

Enumeration Date:

								#	
									Name of Street
									House Number
								1	Dwelling Number
								2	Family Number
								3	Name of each person whose place of abode on June 1, 1900 was in this family.
								4	Relationship to head of household
								5	Color
								6	Sex
								7	Month and year of birth
								8	Age at last birthday
								9	Single, widowed, married, divorced
								10	# of years married
								11	Mother of how many children
								12	# of children living
								13	Birthplace of this person
								14	Birthplace of father
								15	Birthplace of mother
								16	Year of immigration
								17	# years in the US
								18	Naturalized citizen
								19	Occupation of everyone over 10 years
								20	# months not employed
								21	# months attended school this year
								22	Can read
								23	Can write
								24	Speaks English
								25	Owned or rented
								26	Owned free or mortgaged
								27	Farm or house
								28	No. of farm schedule

1910 U.S. Federal Census

State:

County:

City:

Page:

Enumeration District:

Call #/URL:

Enumeration Date:

										Name of Street
										House Number
									1	Dwelling Number
									2	Family Number
									3	Name of each person whose place of abode on June 1, 1910 was in this family.
									4	Relationship to head of household
									5	Sex
									6	Color
									7	Age at last birthday
									8	Single, widowed, married, divorced
									9	# of years of present marriage
									10	Mother of how many children
									11	# of children living
									12	Birthplace of this person
									13	Birthplace of father
									14	Birthplace of mother
									15	Year of immigration
									16	Naturalized or alien
									17	Speaks English, if not give language spoken
									18 & 19	Occupation & nature of business
									20	Employer, employee or self emplyed
									21	Out of work on April 15, 1910?
									22	# weeks out of work in 1909
									23	Can read
									24	Can write
									25	Attended school since Sept. 1, 1909
									26	Owned or rented
									27	Owned free or mortgaged
									28	Farm or house
									29	No. of farm schedule
									30	Civil War veteran
									31	Blind
									32	Deaf & Dumb

1910 U.S. Federal Census

State:

County:

City:

Page:

Enumeration District:

Call #/URL:

Enumeration Date:

									Name of Street
									House Number
								1	Dwelling Number
								2	Family Number
								3	Name of each person whose place of abode on June 1, 1910 was in this family.
								4	Relationship to head of household
								5	Sex
								6	Color
								7	Age at last birthday
								8	Single, widowed, married, divorced
								9	# of years of present marriage
								10	Mother of how many children
								11	# of children living
								12	Birthplace of this person
								13	Birthplace of father
								14	Birthplace of mother
								15	Year of immigration
								16	Naturalized or alien
								17	Speaks English, if not give language spoken
								18 & 19	Occupation & nature of business
								20	Employer, employee or self emplyed
								21	Out of work on April 15, 1910?
								22	# weeks out of work in 1909
								23	Can read
								24	Can write
								25	Attended school since Sept. 1, 1909
								26	Owned or rented
								27	Owned free or mortgaged
								28	Farm or house
								29	No. of farm schedule
								30	Civil War veteran
								31	Blind
								32	Deaf & Dumb

								#	
								1	Name of Street
								2	House Number
								3	Dwelling Number
								4	Family Number
								5	Name of each person whose place of abode on June 1, 1920 was in this family.
								6	Relationship to head of household
								7	Home owned or rented
								8	Owned free or mortgaged
								9	Sex
								10	Color
								11	Age at last birthday
								12	Single, widowed, married, divorced
								13	Year of immigration
								14	Naturalized or alien
								15	If naturalized, year of naturalization
								16	Attended school since Sept. 1, 1919
								17	Can read
								18	Can write
								19 & 20	Birthplace of this person, mother tongue
								21 & 22	Birthplace of father, mother tongue
								23 & 24	Birthplace of mother, mother tongue
								25	Speaks English
								26 & 27	Occupation & nature of business
								28	Employer, employee or self emplyed
								29	No. of farm schedule

1920 U.S. Federal Census

State:

County:

City:

Page:

Enumeration District:

Call #/URL:

Enumeration Date

1920 U.S. federal Census

State:

County:

City:

Page:

Enumeration District:

Call #/URL:

Enumeration Date

							1	Name of Street
							2	House Number
							3	Dwelling Number
							4	Family Number
							5	Name of each person whose place of abode on June 1, 1920 was in this family.
							6	Relationship to head of household
							7	Home owned or rented
							8	Owned free or mortgaged
							9	Sex
							10	Color
							11	Age at last birthday
							12	Single, widowed, married, divorced
							13	Year of immigration
							14	Naturalized or alien
							15	If naturalized, year of naturalization
							16	Attended school since Sept. 1, 1919
							17	Can read
							18	Can write
							19 & 20	Birthplace of this person, mother tongue
							21 & 22	Birthplace of father, mother tongue
							23 & 24	Birthplace of mother, mother tongue
							25	Speaks English
							26 & 27	Occupation & nature of business
							28	Employer, employee or self emplyed
							29	No. of farm schedule

1930 U.S. federal Census

State:

County:

City:

Page:

Enumeration District:

Call #/URL:

Enumeration Date:

							#	
							1	Name of Street
							2	House Number
							3	Dwelling Number
							4	Family Number
							5	Name of each person whose place of abode on June 1, 1930 was in this family.
							6	Relationship to head of household
							7	Home owned or rented
							8	Value of home if owned, or monthly rental
							9	Radio set
							10	Live on a farm?
							11	Sex
							12	Color
							13	Age at last birthday
							14	Single, widowed, married, divorced
							15	Age at 1st marriage
							16	Attended school or college since Sept. 1, 1929
							17	Able to read and write
							18	Birthplace of this person
							19	Birthplace of father
							20	Birthplace of mother
							21	Language spoken in home before coming to US
							22	Year of immigration
							23	Naturalized or alien
							24	Speaks English
							25 & 26	Occupation & nature of business
							27	Class of worker
							28	At work? Yes or no
							29	Unemployed line number
							30 & 31	US military veteran? Yes or no, if yes list war.
							32	No. of farm schedule

1930 U.S. Federal Census

State:

County:

City:

Page:

Enumeration District:

Call #/URL:

Enumeration Date:

#		
1	Name of Street	
2	House Number	
3	Dwelling Number	
4	Family Number	
5	Name of each person whose place of abode on June 1, 1930 was in this family.	
6	Relationship to head of household	
7	Home owned or rented	
8	Value of home if owned, or monthly rental	
9	Radio set	
10	Live on a farm?	
11	Sex	
12	Color	
13	Age at last birthday	
14	Single, widowed, married, divorced	
15	Age at 1st marriage	
16	Attended school or college since Sept. 1, 1929	
17	Able to read and write	
18	Birthplace of this person	
19	Birthplace of father	
20	Birthplace of mother	
21	Language spoken in home before coming to US	
22	Year of immigration	
23	Naturalized or alien	
24	Speaks English	
25 & 26	Occupation & nature of business	
27	Class of worker	
28	At work? Yes or no	
29	Unemployed line number	
30 & 31	US military veteran? Yes or no, if yes list war.	
32	No. of farm schedule	

Appendix III. Glossary

Abstract of Title
A set of documents which records the owners of a piece of property through time, and all the recorded instruments and proceedings that affect the title of the property.

Assignment
A document that shows a property owner transferring his or her ownership to another person or company.

Appurtenance
Something belonging to the land and transferred with it, such as buildings, fixtures, rights. It adds to greater enjoyment of the land. A right-of-way is an appurtenance.

Bond
An obligation under seal. (A real estate bond is a written obligation issued on security of a mortgage or deed of trust.)

Consideration
Something of value (usually money) that is given in exchange for a piece of property.

Conveyance
A written instrument, such as a deed or lease, that transfers some ownership interest in real property from one person to another.

Defendant
The party against whom an action is brought in a court of law.

Deed

A formal written instrument by which title to real property is transferred from one owner to another. The deed should contain an accurate description of the property being conveyed, should be signed and witnessed according to the laws of the state where the property is located, and should be delivered to the purchaser at closing day. There are two parties to a deed: the grantor and the grantee. (See also deed of trust, general warranty deed, quitclaim deed, and special warranty deed.)

Deed of Trust

Like a mortgage, a security instrument whereby real property is given as security for a debt. However, in a deed of trust there are three parties to the instrument: the borrower, the trustee, and the lender, (or beneficiary). In such a transaction, the borrower transfers the legal title for the property to the trustee who holds the property in trust as security for the payment of the debt to the lender or beneficiary. If the borrower pays the debt as agreed, the deed of trust becomes void. If, however, he defaults in the payment of the debt, the trustee may sell the property at a public sale, under the terms of the deed of trust. In most jurisdictions where the deed of trust is in force, the borrower is subject to having his property sold without benefit of legal proceedings. A few states have begun in recent years to treat the deed of trust like a mortgage.

Devisee

A person or entity who inherits property in a will.

Devisor

A person or entity who gifts property in a will.

General Warranty Deed

A deed which conveys not only all the grantor's interests in and title to the property to the grantee, but also warrants that if the title is defective (such as mortgage claims, tax liens, title claims, judgments, or mechanic's liens against it) the grantee may hold the grantor liable.

Grantee

That party in the deed who is the buyer or recipient.

Grantor

That party in the deed who is the seller or giver.

Improvement

A structural addition to the land which can be considered to be a fixture.

Indenture

An instrument executed by both grantor and grantee, containing reciprocal agreements, grants or obligations.

Instrument

A legal document.

Land Patent

The transfer of title from a government to the first private owner of a piece of property.

Mechanics Lien

A legal claim placed on property by someone who is owed money for labor, services or supplies contributed to the property for the purpose of improving it.

Mortgage

A temporary, conditional pledge of property to a creditor as security for performance of an obligation or repayment of a debt. The grantor (property owner) gives a mortgage (a promise to repay money) to the grantee (lending institution).

Patentee

The original purchaser of property from the federal government.

Plaintiff

The party who institutes a suit in court.

Plat

A map or chart of a lot, subdivision or community drawn by a surveyor showing boundary lines, buildings, improvements on the land, and easements.

Premises

Land and the improvements on it such as a house, barn, garage, etc. When a deed refers to premises, it does not necessarily mean that a house exists.

Probate

A court proceeding to pass a deceased person's (devisor) property to the heirs (devisee).

Quitclaim Deed

A deed which transfers whatever interest the maker of the deed may have in the particular parcel of land. A quitclaim deed is often given to clear the title when the grantor's interest in a property is questionable. By accepting such a deed the buyer assumes all the risks. Such a deed makes no warranties as to the title, but simply transfers to the buyer whatever interest the grantor has. (See Deed.) A general release of all claims or rights by the grantor to a parcel of land.

Special Warranty Deed

A deed in which the grantor conveys title to the grantee and agrees to protect the grantee against title defects or claims asserted by the grantor and those persons whose right to assert a claim against the title arose during the period the grantor held title to the property. In a special warranty deed the grantor guarantees to the grantee that he has done nothing during the time he held title to the property which has, or which might in the future, impair the grantee's title.

Survey

A map or plat made by a licensed surveyor showing the results of measuring the land with its elevations, improvements, boundaries, and its relationship to surrounding tracts of land. A survey is often required by the lender to insure that a building is actually sited on the land according to its legal description.

Title Search

A search of public records to determine who is the legal owner of the property, and to see if anyone else has any claims in the property via a lien, mortgage, etc.

Warranty Deed

A deed that transfers ownership of real property and in which the grantor guarantees that the title is free and clear of all encumbrances.

Appendix IV. Bibliography

Blumenson, John J. G. *Identifying American Architecture: A Pictorial Guide to Styles and Terms, 1600-1945*. Revised ed. New York: Norton, 1990.

Buhler, Carol Francis. *The House Building: My Search for Its Foundation*. Lawrence, Kan.: Transom Works, 1990.

Dupre, E. *Atlas of the City and County of St. Louis by Congressional District*. Jefferson City, Mo.: Capital City Family Research, 1838.

Fleming, Ann Carter. *St. Louis Family History Research Guide*. St. Louis, Missouri: Fleming Publishing, 2008.

Gravenhorst, Edna. *Historical Home Research in the City of St. Louis*. St. Louis: E. C. Gravenhorst, 2003.

Green, Betsy. *Discovering the History of Your House and Your Neighborhood*. Santa Monica, CA: Santa Monica Press LLC, 2002.

Howe, Barbara J. *Houses and Home: Exploring Their History*. Nashville, Tenn.: AASLH, 1987.

Hugh, Howard. *How Old Is This House?: A Skeleton Key to Dating and Identifying Three Centuries of American Houses*. New York, NY: Home Renovation Association, 1989.

continued next page

Hutawa, Julius. *Atlas of the County of St. Louis, MO*. St. Louis: Julius Hutawa [1847].

Johnson, B.F. *Atlas of St. Louis County, 1893*.

Klein, Marilyn W. & David P. Fogle. *Clues to American Architecture*. Starrhill Press: Washington, DC, 1986.

Kyvig, David E. and Myron A. Marty. *Nearby History: Exploring the Past Around You*. Walnut Creek, Calif.: AltaMira Press, 1996.

Light, Sally. *House Histories: A Guide to Tracing the Genealogy of Your Home*. Spencertown, N.Y.: Golden Hill Press, 1989.

McAlester, Virginia and Lee McAlester. *A Field Guide to American Houses*. New York: Alfred A. Knopf, 1997.

Morgan, James. *If These Walls Had Ears: The Biography of a House*. New York: Warner Books, 1996.

Phillips, Stephen J. *Old House Dictionary*. Washington, DC: Preservation Press, 1994.

Pitzman, Julius. *Pitzman's Atlas of the City and County of St. Louis Missouri, 1878*. Philadelphia, PA: A.B. Holcombe & Co.

Plat Book of St. Louis County, Missouri, 1909 Compiled from County Records and Actual Surveys. Des Moines, Iowa: Northwest Publications, 1909.

Rifkind, Carole. *A Field Guide to Contemporary American Architecture.* New York: Dutton, 1998.

Savage, Charles. *Architecture of the private streets of St. Louis: the architects and the houses they designed.* Columbia: University of Missouri, 1987.

Scharf, J. Thomas. *History of Saint Louis City and County from the earliest periods to the present day: including biographical sketches of representative men.* Philadelphia: L.H. Everts, 1883.

St. Louis Plat and Record Co. Atlas of St. Louis County. 1909.

Thomas, William Lyman. *History of St. Louis County Missouri.* St. Louis, Mo.: Clarke, 1911.

Zehr, Alison. *Your House Has a History: A Step-by-Step Guide to Researching Your Property.* Chicago, IL: City of Chicago, Dept. of Planning and Development, 1998.

Additional Web Sites

http://www.myhousehistory.net

http://www.cyndislist.com/houses.htm

http://www.cyndislist.com/land.htm

http://www.oldhousehistory.com

http://www.familysearch.org

http://www.ancestry.com

Unlocking My House History

Unraveling the mysteries of a Century Home can require real detective work

by Kim Wolterman

When Jim and I purchased our 1902 aging beauty on South Maple Avenue in 1987, we knew that we would seek the designation of Century Home from the Webster Groves Historical Society.

In 2001 I began the arduous task of researching the history of the home. A call to the Historical Society led to the information that two pieces of documentation written at the time the house was constructed would be required to show the year the house had been built, and for whom. A caution was issued that St. Louis County property tax records are not always accurate. Hence the year 1902 might not be correct.

My search began with the book *How to Research the History of Your Webster Groves House* by Ann Morris, available at the Webster Groves Library. While offering some sound advice, the book was published in 1980. In this day and age of computerized records and the Internet, a lot of things have changed since the book was released.

Countless trips to the St. Louis County Recorder of Deeds office led to copies of deeds on the property all the way back to May 26, 1886, when Mary A. Shepley sold 20 acres of land to Alexander Russell. The property was subdivided into 17 lots, which became Alexander Russell's Subdivision.

While the deeds were great to have and contained a good deal of information, none of them specifically indicated that a house was located on the land.

With a list of all the property owners in hand, a review of the Webster Groves tax records was done. These records begin with tax year 1897, as Webster incorporated in 1896, and are now available on microfilm at the Webster Groves Public Library. They are an excellent source of supporting documentation.

The tax records matched our property owners of record for each year, but the amount of tax paid did not make a drastic jump until the 1904 tax book. Keep in mind that the property changed hands in April of 1902, so any construction would not show up until the property was assessed in 1903, and paid in 1904. So was the house built in 1902 or 1903?

A search of the Kate Moody file of Webster Groves history, city and county directories, census records, Webster Groves tax records, Webster Groves church records, materials at the Webster Groves and Missouri Historical Societies, and published books on Webster Groves yielded no further clues.

Meetings with architects who specialize in old buildings and Esley Hamilton of the St. Louis County Parks Department provided guidelines on dating a structure, but nothing specific enough to narrow down the year to 1902. Real estate tax records at St. Louis County, which would have been helpful in identifying a year when the taxes jumped dramatically, are only available for the last 25 years. Older records have been destroyed.

I had hit a brick wall. So I decided to take a different approach. An avid genealogist, I put my genealogical skills to work. A search on the Internet for Claude A. Morton, who purchased the property in 1902, hit pay dirt.

Holly Ann Burt, great-granddaughter of Claude and Jessie Morton, had a website listing her family tree. Upon exchanging emails it was determined that her ancestors had actually lived

Through her research, Kim Wolterman discovered that Claude Morton, for whom her house was built, was very active in business and civic organizations. Mr. Morton served as a Webster Groves alderman and was the chairman of the Library Board.

in Webster Groves in the early 1900s. Holly had inherited her grandmother Aline's records, including diaries and photos. She emailed me some house photos that were indeed early photos of the house at 213 S. Maple Avenue.

The photos showed a stable in the side yard, a cook house out back and Maple Avenue as a dirt road with wooden sidewalks. Exciting as all this was, it still wasn't known when the house was built.

In August of 2005, I met with Holly at her home in Chicago and poured through old family documents. Holly's grandmother, Aline, had compiled unique photo albums that contained not only pictures but newspaper clippings, articles about Webster Groves High School, and goings-on around town. They are a fascinating snapshot of Webster Groves at the turn of the century.

Photos in the album show the family having tea in the back yard, entertaining friends on the front porch and enjoying picnics at the Meramec Highlands. The Mortons raised four children in Webster Groves. Additional snapshots show Webster Groves High School students singing with other area students on Art Hill in Forest Park in 1916. Photos with friends in front of the high

school, piano recitals, and gatherings with other young people on lawns around town gave me a rare opportunity to see life in our community back when the neighborhoods were new.

But most importantly to my research, Aline had typed up an obituary for her father, Claude, upon his death in 1953. In it she wrote that "the Mortons lived for 36 years in the house they built at 213 S. Maple Avenue in Webster Groves."

This corresponds with the fact that the Mortons sold their home on Maple Avenue in 1938. Further, the obituary provided insights into the life of Claude Morton. In addition to being a partner in Morton & Co., grain commissioner, Claude was very active in business and civic organizations.

He served as secretary-treasurer, vice president and president of the St. Louis Clearing House Association, secretary and treasurer of the American Buff Plymouth Rock Club, and was a member of the executive committee of the American Poultry Association. He was also a Webster Groves alderman and chairman of the Library Board.

The family was active in First Congregational Church in Webster Groves.

Upon submission of a completed application to the Webster Groves Historical Society, including Deeds of Trust on the property, old photos of the house and the original family along with the obituary, we received our Century Home plaque in 2005.

Only the third family to live in the house, my completed house history provides a link from the past to the present.

So, is the research done? Not quite. The Mortons purchased the property from noted St. Louis architect George D. Barnett, designer of the Cathedral Basilica of St. Louis as well as other notable landmarks in the city. Was he the architect for the house at 213. S. Maple Avenue? Stay tuned!

Who's Been Sleeping in My Bed(room)?

Researching a St. Louis
County, Missouri Home
by Kim Wolterman

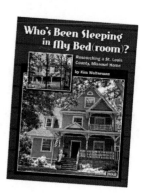

Book Order Form

Person placing order: _____

Ship order to (if other than person placing order): _____

Address line 1: _____

Address line 2: _____

City, State, ZIP: _____

Email address: _____

Phone number: (_____) _____

Number of copies _____ x $16.95 + $5.00 each for tax and shipping.

Total amount of payment enclosed with this order $_____

If you would like a message inscribed (all books ordered using this form are signed by the author) PRINT clearly the inscription message on the back of this order form. Great gift idea!

Make check payable and mail to:

Provenance Publishing LLC
213 S. Maple Ave.
St. Louis, MO 63119
314-283-4605

Books may also be ordered online at **www.provenancepublishing.net,** with payment through PayPal.